Fargo Moorhead AM Rotary Club
www.fmrotary.org

Presented to the
Fargo Public Children's Library

In honor of

[signature]

Club Officer: LARRY Ornberg, Pres

Dated this 2nd day of MAY, 2013.

Pet Corner / Rincón de las mascotas

MARVELOUS MICE/ RATONES MARAVILLOSOS

By Rose Carraway

Traducción al español: Eduardo Alamán

Gareth Stevens Publishing

Please visit our website, www.garethstevens.com. For a free color catalog of all our high-quality books, call toll free 1-800-542-2595 or fax 1-877-542-2596.

Library of Congress Cataloging-in-Publication Data

Carraway, Rose.
 Marvelous mice = Ratones maravillosos / Rose Carraway.
    p. cm. — (Pet corner = Rincón de las mascotas)
 Includes index.
 ISBN 978-1-4339-6643-9 (library binding)
 1. Mice as pets—Juvenile literature. I. Title. II. Title: Ratones maravillosos.
 SF459.M5C3718 2012
 636.935'3—dc23
                                           2011026956

First Edition

Published in 2012 by
Gareth Stevens Publishing
111 East 14th Street, Suite 349
New York, NY 10003

Copyright © 2012 Gareth Stevens Publishing

Editor: Katie Kawa
Designer: Andrea Davison-Bartolotta
Spanish Translation: Eduardo Alamán

Photo credits: Cover David De Lossy/Photodisc/Thinkstock; pp. 1, 21, 24 (lettuce) iStockphoto/Thinkstock; pp. 5, 11, 15, 19, 21, 23, 24 (lettuce, pellets) Shutterstock.com; pp. 7, 9, 13 iStockphoto.com; pp. 17, 24 (paws) Bob Elsdale/The Image Bank/Getty Images.

All rights reserved. No part of this book may be reproduced in any form without permission in writing from the publisher, except by a reviewer.

Printed in the United States of America

CPSIA compliance information: Batch #CW12GS: For further information contact Gareth Stevens, New York, New York at 1-800-542-2595.

Contents

Playtime 4
Furry Friends 12
Time to Eat 18
Words to Know .24
Index. 24

- -

Contenido

A jugar 4
Amigos peludos .12
Hora de comer 18
Palabras que debes saber 24
Índice 24

Mice like to run!

¡A los ratones les gusta correr!

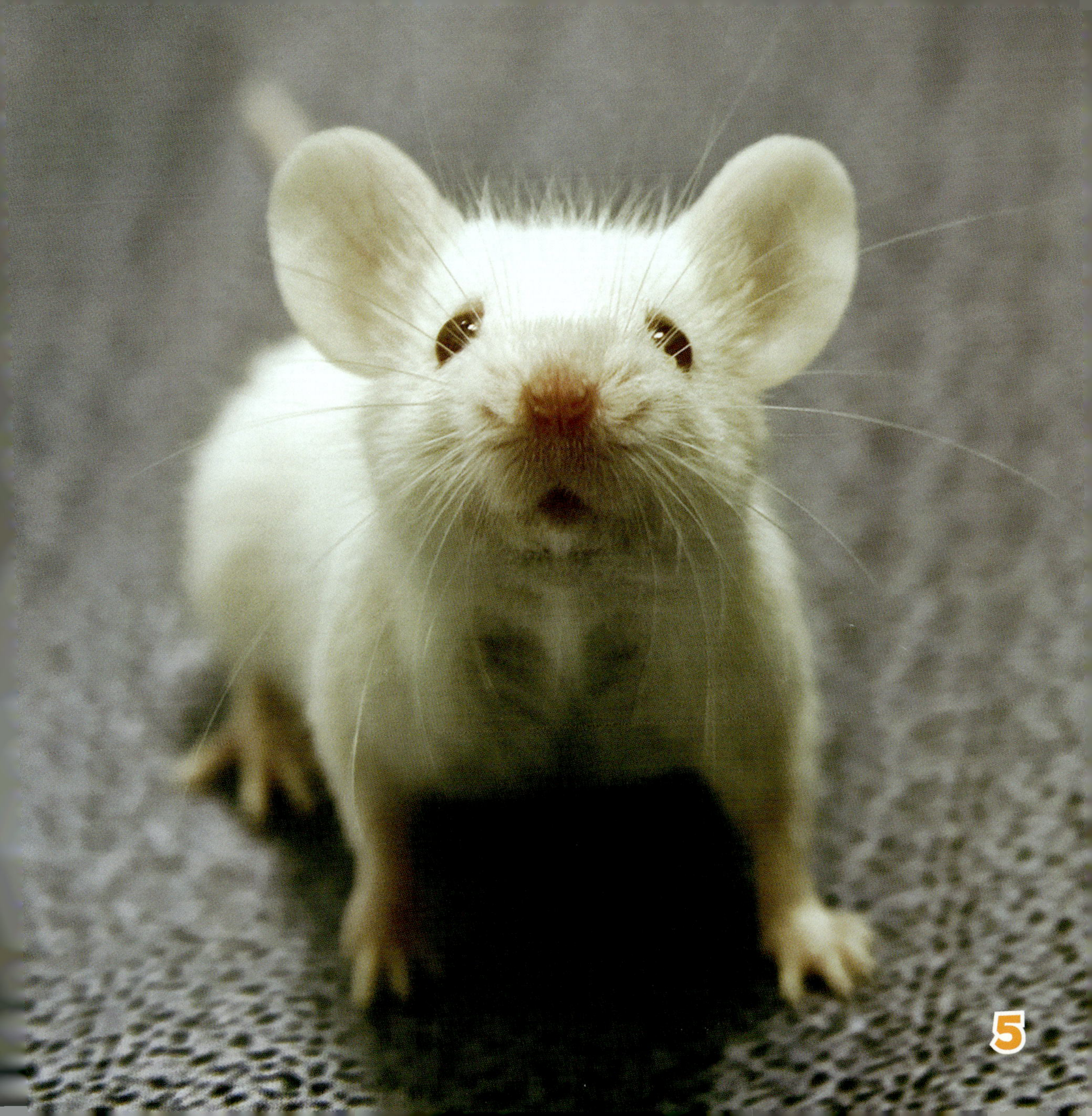

A pet mouse has
a wheel in its cage.
It runs in the wheel.

Los ratones mascota
tienen una rueda en su
jaula. ¡A los ratones
les gusta correr en
la rueda!

7

A mouse has toys to chew. This keeps its teeth healthy.

Un ratón tiene juguetes para morder. Así mantiene los dientes sanos.

9

Mice sleep during the day. They play at night.

Los ratones duermen durante el día. Juegan durante la noche.

11

Most pet mice are white.

La mayoría de los ratones mascota son blancos.

13

Fancy mice are special pet mice. They come in lots of colors!

Los ratones de fantasía son mascotas especiales. ¡Tienen muchos colores!

15

Mice clean themselves.
They lick their paws
and wipe their fur.

Los ratones se lavan
a sí mismos. Se lamen
las patas y se limpian
el pelaje.

17

Pet mice eat food called pellets. These come from the pet store.

Los ratones mascota comen una comida especial llamada "pellets."

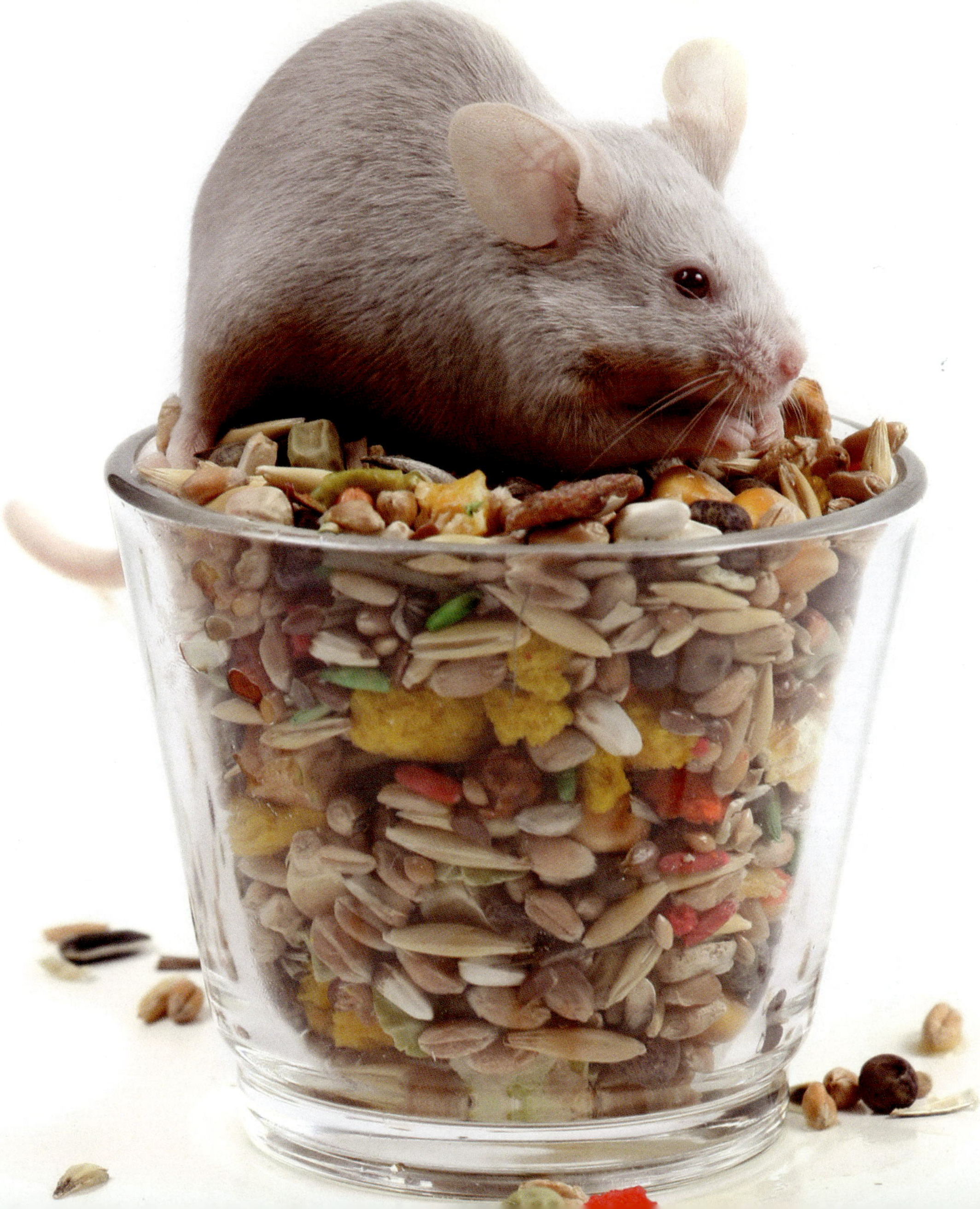

Mice eat green vegetables too. They like lettuce.

Los ratones también comen verduras. Les gusta la lechuga.

21

Mice learn tricks. They sit in a person's hand!

Los ratones aprenden trucos. ¡Se pueden sentar en las manos de las personas!

23

Words to Know/
Palabras que debes saber

lettuce /
(la) lechuga

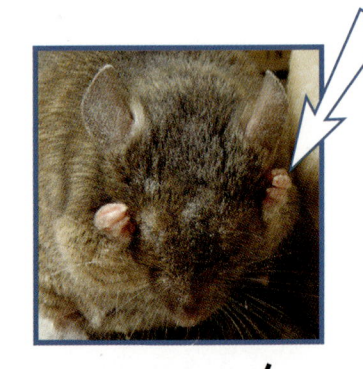

paws /
(las) patas

pellets /
(los) pellets

Index / Índice

eat/comer 18, 20

fancy mice/(los) ratones
de fantasía 14

tricks/(los) trucos 22

wheel/(la) rueda 6